Explorers

Robots
Chris Oxlade

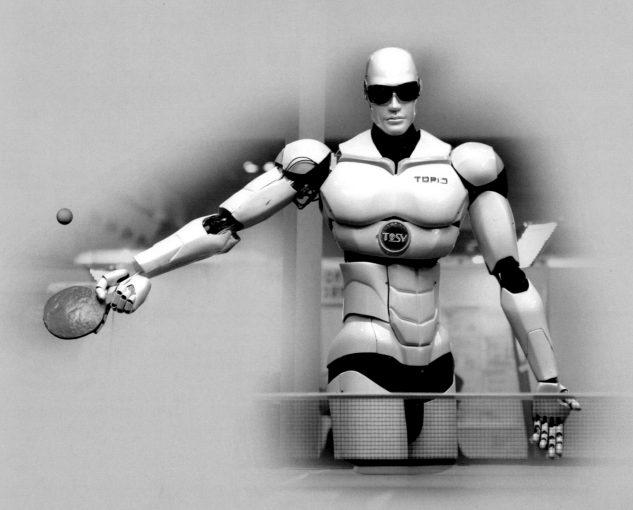

KINGFISHER
NEW YORK

KINGFISHER
LONDON & NEW YORK

Copyright © Kingfisher 2013
Published in the United States by Kingfisher,
175 Fifth Ave., New York, NY 10010
Kingfisher is an imprint of Macmillan Children's Books, London.
All rights reserved.

Illustrations by: Peter Bull Art Studio

Distributed in the U.S. and Canada by Macmillan, 175 Fifth
Ave., New York, NY 10010

Library of Congress Cataloging-in-Publication data
has been applied for.

ISBN: 978-0-7534-6816-6

Kingfisher books are available for special promotions and
premiums. For details contact: Special Markets Department,
Macmillan, 175 Fifth Ave., New York, NY 10010.

For more information, please visit
www.kingfisherbooks.com

Printed in China
1 3 5 7 9 8 6 4 2
1TR/0313/UTD/WKT/140MA

Picture credits

**The Publisher would like to thank the following
for permission to reproduce their material.
(t = top, b = bottom, c = center, l = left, r = right):**
Cover Getty/Adrian Dennis and pages 1 Alamy/AlamyCelebrity;
2tl Science Photo Library(SPL)/James King-Holmes; 4l SPL/
Maximilian Stock Ltd.; 4r SPL/James King-Holmes; 5tl DLR
Institute of Robotics & Machatronics/German Aerospace Center;
5tr Corbis/YM Yik/epa; 5cr SPL/Louise Murray; 5b Rex Features/
MCP; 6tl Willow Garage Inc., Menlo Park, California; 8tl Getty/
Koichi Kamoshida; 8cl Corbis/Toru Hanai//Reuters; 8cr WowWee
Technologies; 9t Getty/AFP; 9bl Getty/Yoshikazu Tsuno/AFP;
9br Getty/Yoshikazu Tsuno/AFP; 10bl Alamy/Doug Perrine;
12 Robovolc, A Robot for Volcano Exploration, Prof. Muscato,
Dept. of Integrated Electronic Systems, University of Catania,
Italy; 12tr Getty/Chip Somodevilla; 13tl Getty/Ethan Miller;
13tr Liquid Robotics, Moffett Park, California; 13cl Atlantic
Emergency Solutions, USA; 13b IFE/URI/NOAA; 14tl iRobot
Corporation; 16l The RobotCub Consortium; 16tr PA Archive/
Press Association Images; 16br Getty/Yoshikazu Tsuno/AFP;
17ct PA Archive/Press Association Images; 17cl PA Archive/
Press Association Images; 17b Getty/Junko Kimura; 18bl NASA/
JPL; 20cr NASA/JPL; 20bl NASA/JPL; 21t NASA/JPL; 21cr NASA/
JSC Engineers; 21b Rex Features/KeystoneUSA-Zuma; 24tl
SPL/DPA; 24tr Alamy/Christopher Honeywell; 25tl Getty/Asahi
Shimbun; 25cr Getty/Toru Yamanaka; 25b SPL/Peter Menzel;
26bl Tosy Robotics JS Company, Vietnam; 28tr Getty/Yoshikazu
Tsuno/AFP; 28bl Getty/AFP; 28br Getty/Koichi Kamoshida; 29tl
Getty/Yoshikazu Tsuno/AFP; 29tr Getty/Adrian Dennis; 29bl
Getty/Bloomberg; 29br Rex Features/South West News Service;
30tl Corbis/Ralph White; 30tr Alamy/RIA Novosti; 30ctl Alamy/
Art Directors TRIP; 30cbr NASA/JPL; 30bl DARPA, U.S. Dept.
of Defense; 31tl Getty/Science & Society Picture; 31tr Press
Association/AP; 31ctl IFM-Geomar, University of Kiel Germany;
31ctr NASA/JPL; Shutterstock/Maksim Dubinsky; 31cbr Rex
Features/Fisheries and Oceans, Canada; 31bl European Space
Agency/NASA; 31br Rex Features/RoboDynamics/Schultzworks

Contents

More to explore

On some of the pages in this book, you will find colored buttons with symbols on them. There are four different colors, and each belongs to a different topic. Choose a topic, follow its colored buttons through the book, and you'll make some interesting discoveries of your own.

For example, on page 7 you'll find an orange button, like this, next to a robot. The orange buttons are about future robots.

Page 23

Future

There is a page number in the button. Turn to that page (page 23) to find an orange button next to another robot. Follow all the steps through the book, and at the end of your journey you'll find out how the steps are linked and discover even more information about this topic.

Science

History

Technology

The other topics in this book are science, history, and technology. Follow the steps and see what you can discover!

All about robots

Robots are amazing machines that can work on their own. They carry out a huge range of jobs in a huge range of places, from painting cars in factories to exploring planets in space.

Robots have gripping tools to hold on to things. Electric motors close the gripper, and electronic sensors prevent the gripper from crushing objects.

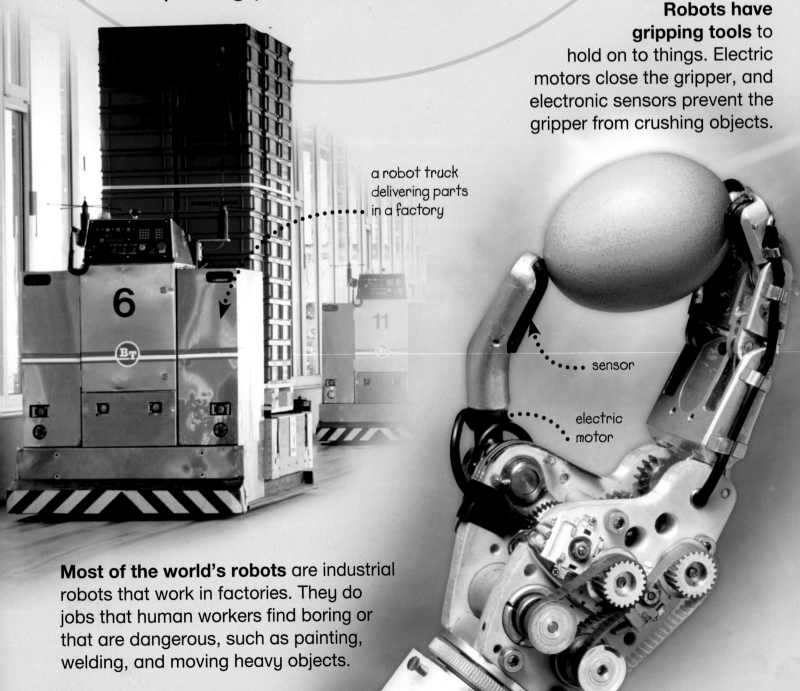

a robot truck delivering parts in a factory

sensor

electric motor

Most of the world's robots are industrial robots that work in factories. They do jobs that human workers find boring or that are dangerous, such as painting, welding, and moving heavy objects.

humanoid
robot "Justin"

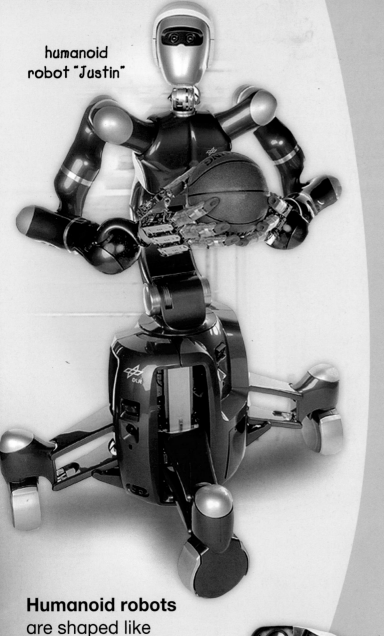

Bomb disposal is a perfect job for robots because it is so dangerous. These robots are remote-controlled machines with tools to make explosive devices safe.

Humanoid robots are shaped like humans. Some humanoids can even walk. An android is a robot that looks like a human.

WALL•E is a fictional garbage-collecting robot.

Fictional robots in movies are more advanced than today's robots, although some of the real robots you willl find in this book might look a little like them.

Page 19

What is this?

1. Windoro robot cleaning the windows

2. LawnBott robot cutting the grass

3. recharging station for the Roomba robot

Robots at home

Robots that work in homes are called domestic robots. They help with chores such as cleaning and gardening—stopping only to recharge their batteries. The robot housekeepers are just experimental, but the other helpful robots already exist in some homes.

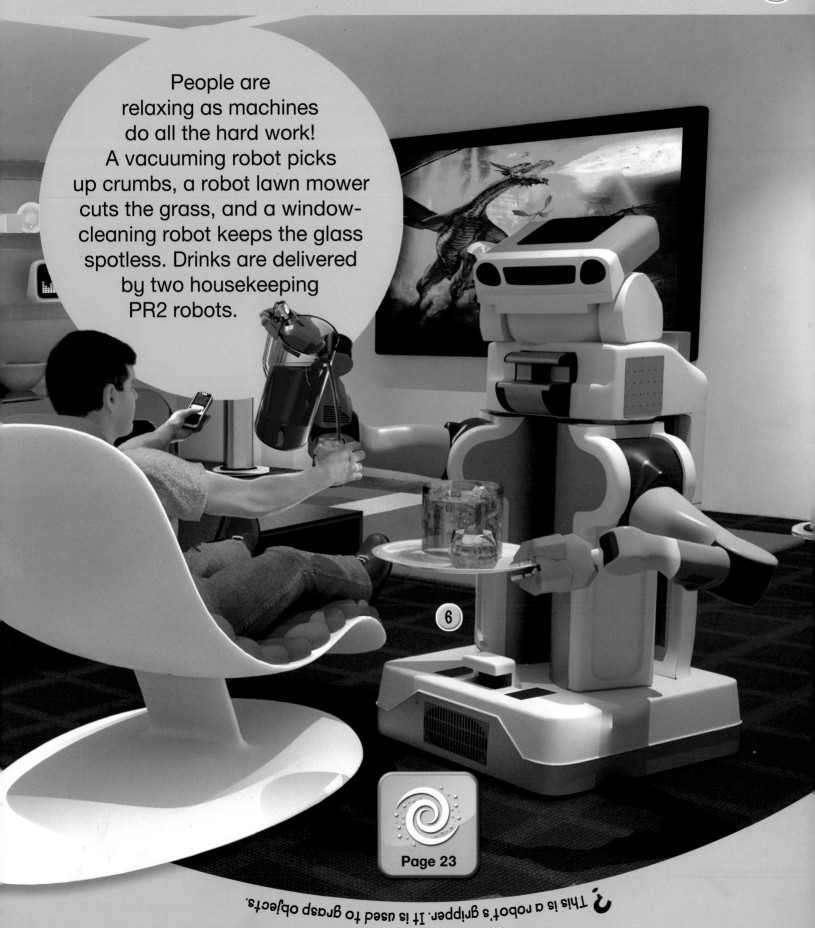

People are relaxing as machines do all the hard work! A vacuuming robot picks up crumbs, a robot lawn mower cuts the grass, and a window-cleaning robot keeps the glass spotless. Drinks are delivered by two housekeeping PR2 robots.

6

Page 23

¿ This is a robot's gripper. It is used to grasp objects.

Learn about the science of robotics with robot construction toys. Kits contain sensors and motors and are programmed through a personal computer.

Lego Mindstorms NXT kit

Rovio keeps an eye on your home using a webcam.

PaPeRo is designed to entertain young children. It can talk, dance, and play games—and is even ticklish!

Around the house

There are domestic robots for entertainment, play, home security, and even for doing chores. All of these robots are dedicated to one job. There are hardly any multipurpose robots that can do several different jobs around the home.

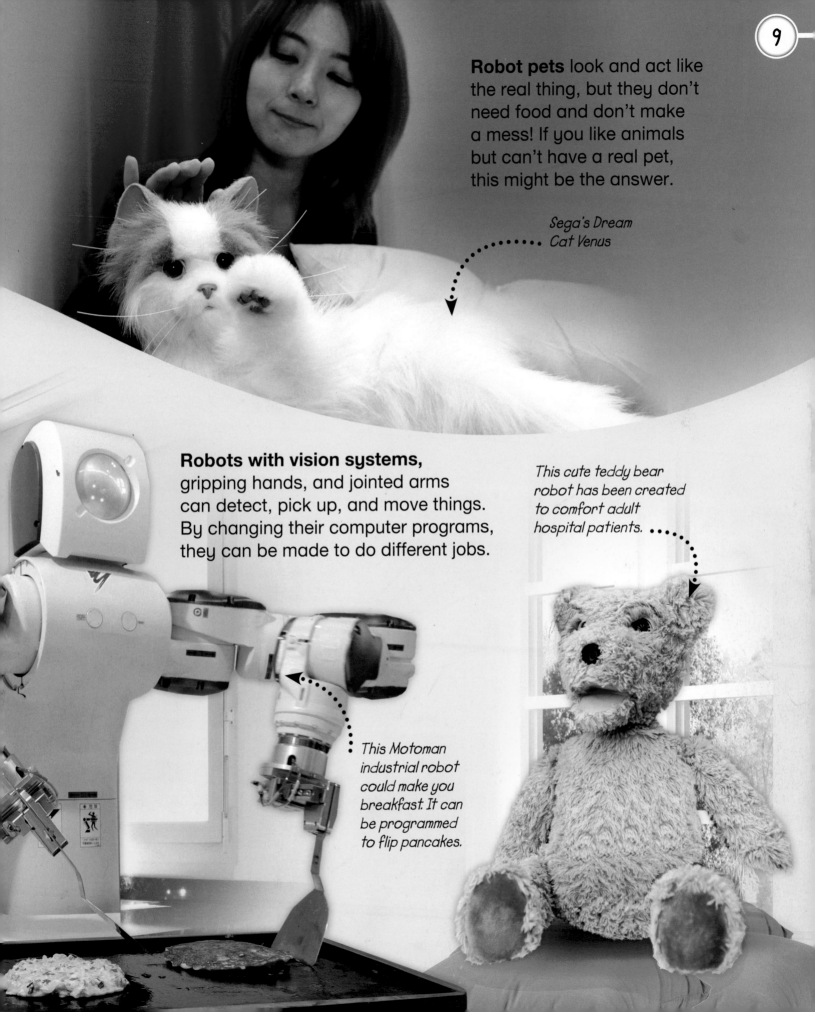

Robot pets look and act like the real thing, but they don't need food and don't make a mess! If you like animals but can't have a real pet, this might be the answer.

Sega's Dream Cat Venus

Robots with vision systems, gripping hands, and jointed arms can detect, pick up, and move things. By changing their computer programs, they can be made to do different jobs.

This cute teddy bear robot has been created to comfort adult hospital patients.

This Motoman industrial robot could make you breakfast. It can be programmed to flip pancakes.

Underwater exploration

The depths of the oceans are hostile places for humans because of the immense water pressure. Robot submersibles (small submarines) are used to explore these dark deep-sea areas because they are not affected by the pressure.

Page 14

Below the surface of the Atlantic Ocean are two autonomous underwater vehicles (AUVs). One is taking photographs, and the other is mapping the ocean floor. Nearby, a remotely operated vehicle (ROV) cruises among thermal vents. It photographs the strange creatures living in the pitch-black water.

What is this?

1 autonomous underwater vehicle (AUV)

2 Dumbo octopus

3 robot arm grabbing samples of rocks

? This is an anglerfish. It attracts prey with a glowing light.

Page 18

Page 30

4 Video cameras in the vehicle send images to the surface.

5 thermal vent on the ocean floor

6 Nereus, a remotely operated vehicle (ROV)

Dangerous jobs

Robots work in dangerous environments, from the ocean depths to volcanic craters. Some are remotely controlled—by a person using a radio or through a cable. Others are autonomous, which means they are able to work by themselves.

Active volcanoes can be dangerous places for volcano scientists, called volcanologists. Robovolc is designed to drive into roasting-hot craters to measure the temperature and analyze volcanic gases.

This AirRobot helicopter is a spy in the sky.

ROBOVOLC
http://www.robovolc.dees.unict.it

MQ-9 Reaper

A video camera sends images to a pilot on the ground.

solar panels

Unmanned aerial vehicles (UAVs), or "drones," are robot aircraft without a pilot onboard. They are used mainly for military spying but also for collecting scientific data from the atmosphere.

Surface robots, such as Wave Glider, cruise for months across the oceans collecting data, including temperature and water quality, and transmitting it via satellite. Power comes from wave motion and solar panels.

LUF60 is used when it's too dangerous for human firefighters.

Remotely operated vehicles (ROVs) are controlled from the surface by a signal sent down a cable. Video signals from the ROV's cameras travel up the cable so the operator can see where the ROV is going.

ROV Hercules taking photographs of the Titanic shipwreck.

What is this?

1 small unmanned ground vehicle (SUGV) with tracks

2 surveillance video camera

3 operator controlling the SUGV

Page 30

Page 27

Robots on patrol

Mobile robots move across the ground on tracks, wheels, or legs. Tracks and wheels spread out a robot's weight and grip the ground well. Legs are good for very rough or steep terrain, but making a robot walk without falling over is very tricky.

These robots are helping with a rescue mission. A tracked robot carries an injured person, while two walking robots move heavy safety equipment over rocky ground with ease. Ahead of them a robot checks for hazards, sending images to its human operator.

This is the video camera on an SUGV. It sends images to the robot's operator.

Moving parts

Robots have moving parts, such as arms. These are connected by joints that are powered by actuators. Cameras and sensors send data to the robot's computer so that it knows when to turn the actuators on and off, moving the joints.

Hexapod robots move using their six legs.

Actuators are like muscles, helping robots move, grip, and lift things. They can be electric, hydraulic (liquid powered), or pneumatic (air powered).

The iCub has 53 electric motors.

This robot, the ACM-R5, slithers like a real snake.

Each finger is moved by a separate motor.

Bipedal robots walk on two legs, like a human. They can walk almost anywhere, including up and down stairs. To enable them to do this, they must have a sense of balance.

A robot car during the DARPA Grand Challenge.

The DARPA Grand Challenge is a contest for robot researchers. Competitors must build an autonomous car that can drive itself around a course without hitting other cars. Crashes do happen, though!

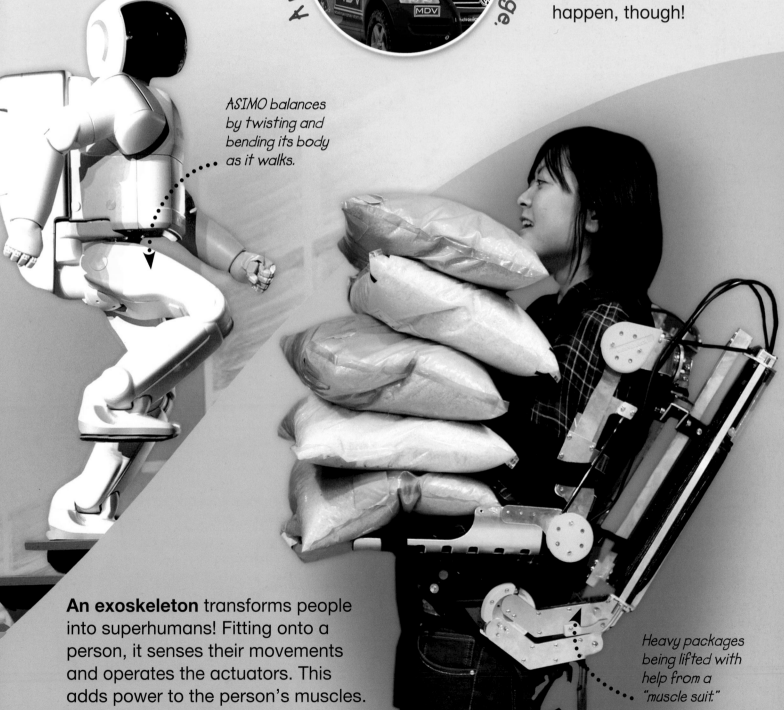

ASIMO balances by twisting and bending its body as it walks.

An exoskeleton transforms people into superhumans! Fitting onto a person, it senses their movements and operates the actuators. This adds power to the person's muscles.

Heavy packages being lifted with help from a "muscle suit."

Space exploration

We have robots to thank for most of our knowledge of the solar system. Robot spacecraft called probes have visited the Moon and all of the planets, including Mars. Journeys can take months or even years. Some probes descend to the surface to carry out experiments.

Page 14

The car-size Curiosity rover is a mobile laboratory. It is exploring the surface of Mars and carrying out experiments. It is examining a Martian rock using its powerful laser. In the background is the craft that lowered Curiosity safely onto the planet's surface.

What are these?

Page 22

1 Curiosity's landing system

2 The Martian surface is scattered with rocks.

3 Curiosity rover

These are rocks on the surface of Mars.

Page 23

Page 30

4 mast with a laser, cameras, and a telescope

5 robot arm for close-up investigation of rocks

6 six aluminum wheels, each with its own motor

Working in space

Robots are good machines for the space environment. Unlike human astronauts, they don't need life support such as food, water, and air—just a supply of electricity! They visit other planets and work on space stations.

scientists working on Juno, the Jupiter-bound probe, in 2011

Huge radio dishes are needed to communicate with robot spacecraft (probes). Commands are sent to the probes as radio signals. The dish also collects weak signals coming from probes out in space. These signals carry images and other data.

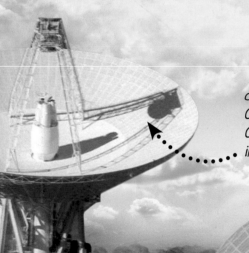

a radio dish at Canberra Deep Space Communication Complex in Australia

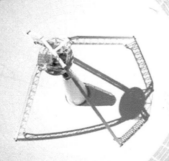

Robot probes that travel to other planets are complex machines. They have delicate instruments onboard and can take years to design and build.

Spirit rover on Mars

a robot arm scooping up a sample of Martian soil

Robot landers and rovers often have robot arms, which are just like the arms of robots that work on Earth. Probe arms move different tools and sensors to where they are needed.

NASA designed the soccerball-size, free-flying AERCam robot to inspect the outside of the International Space Station and send images back to the crew.

Robonaut 2 is a humanoid robot that has been created to help astronauts working on the International Space Station. It is designed to do simple jobs, such as holding tools and materials for the astronauts, both inside the station and on space walks outside.

What is this?

1 Computers control all of the robots.

2 autonomous delivery vehicle carrying parts

3 hydraulic actuators for moving joints

Page 27

Robot workers

Most of the world's robots are industrial robots. They work in factories, moving objects from place to place and operating tools such as drills, wrenches, and welding guns. They repeat the same task over and over with accuracy, and they never get tired.

Page 11

Page 18

As car bodies move along the production line, industrial robots are hard at work. They are adding parts, tightening bolts, welding metal, and spray-painting. Autonomous robot vehicles bring parts from a warehouse, following magnetic tracks on the floor.

This is a spray gun. It is used by a robot arm to paint objects such as cars.

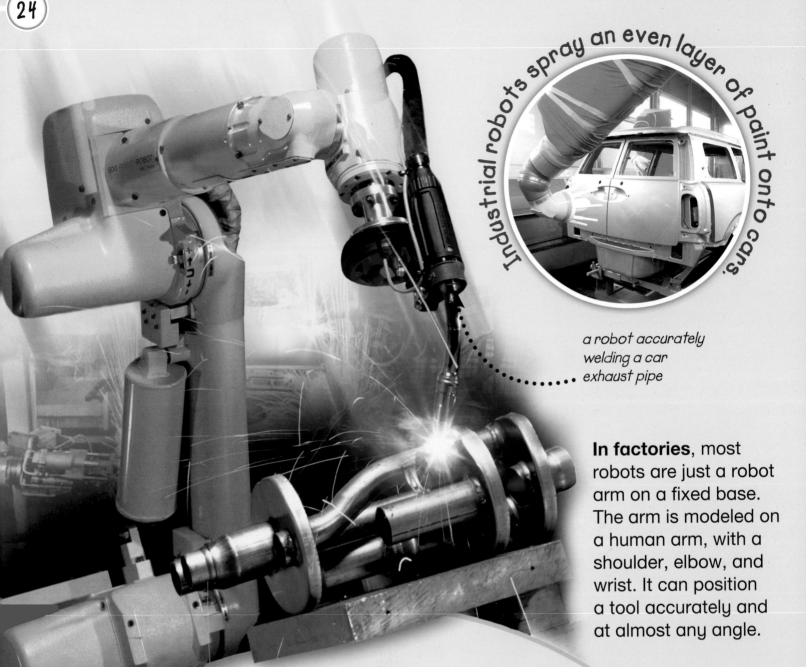

Industrial robots spray an even layer of paint onto cars.

a robot accurately welding a car exhaust pipe

In factories, most robots are just a robot arm on a fixed base. The arm is modeled on a human arm, with a shoulder, elbow, and wrist. It can position a tool accurately and at almost any angle.

Industrial jobs

Robots do all sorts of jobs in factories. Equipping a robot arm with different tools, such as grippers and screwdrivers, enables it to do a range of tasks. Industrial robots also work on farms and in hospitals and laboratories.

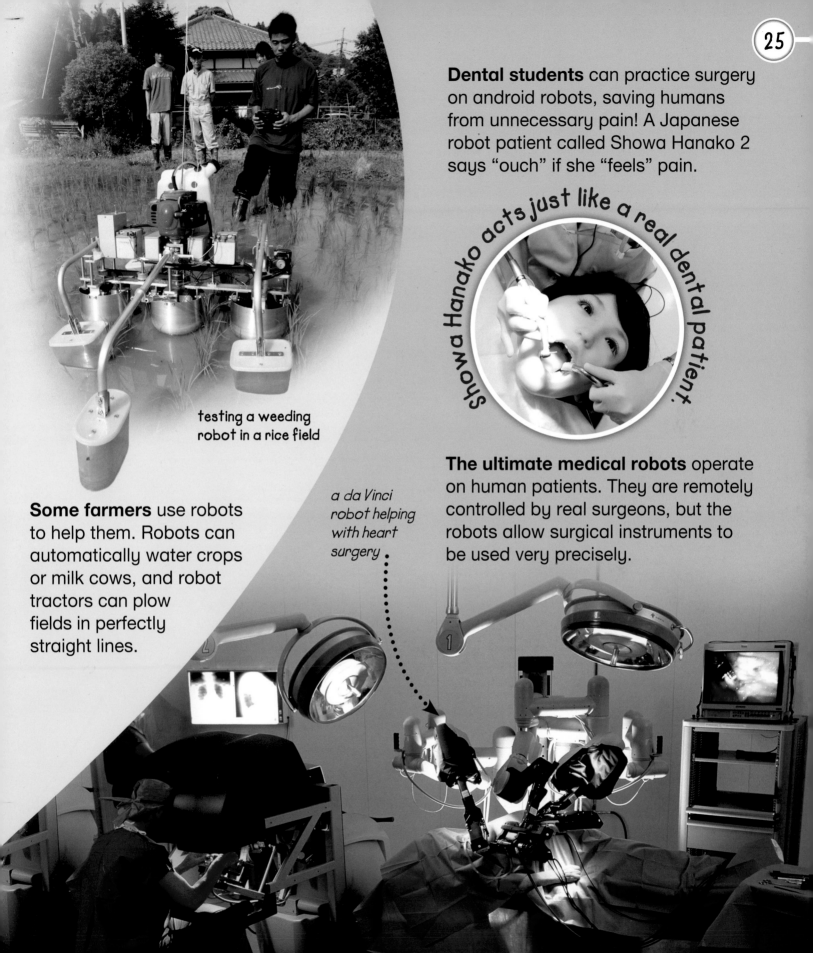

Dental students can practice surgery on android robots, saving humans from unnecessary pain! A Japanese robot patient called Showa Hanako 2 says "ouch" if she "feels" pain.

Showa Hanako acts just like a real dental patient.

testing a weeding robot in a rice field

Some farmers use robots to help them. Robots can automatically water crops or milk cows, and robot tractors can plow fields in perfectly straight lines.

a da Vinci robot helping with heart surgery

The ultimate medical robots operate on human patients. They are remotely controlled by real surgeons, but the robots allow surgical instruments to be used very precisely.

Humanoids and androids

Humanoids and androids are types of robots.
A humanoid has a body, head, arms, and legs
like a human but still looks like a machine.
An android is designed to look and act
like a human, with a realistic face
and human behavior.

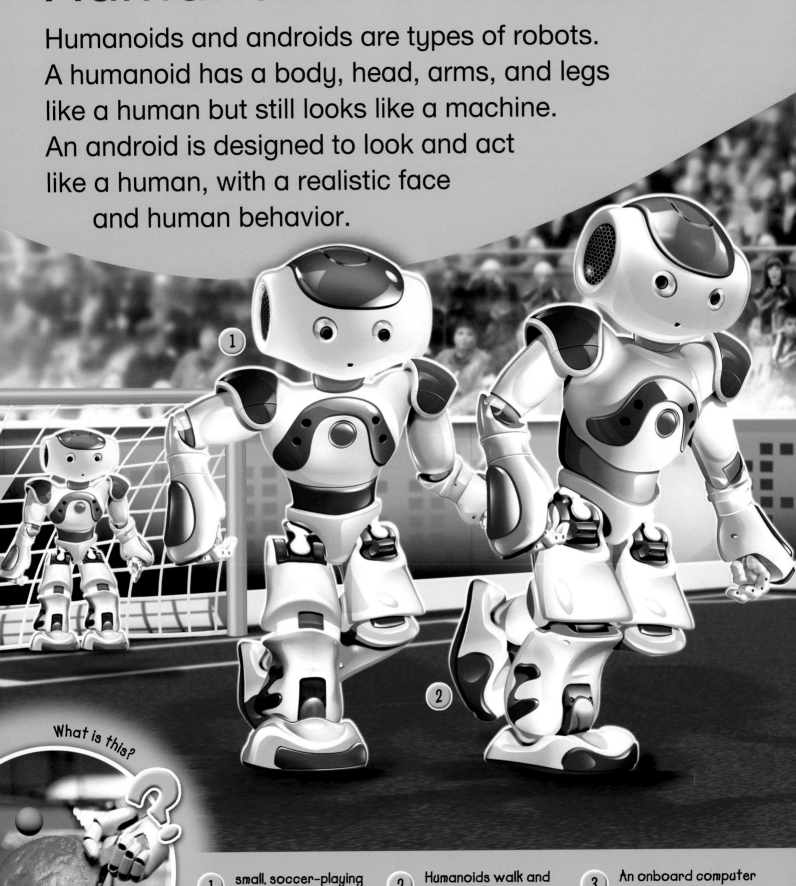

What is this?

1 small, soccer-playing humanoid robots

2 Humanoids walk and run on two legs.

3 An onboard computer controls movement.

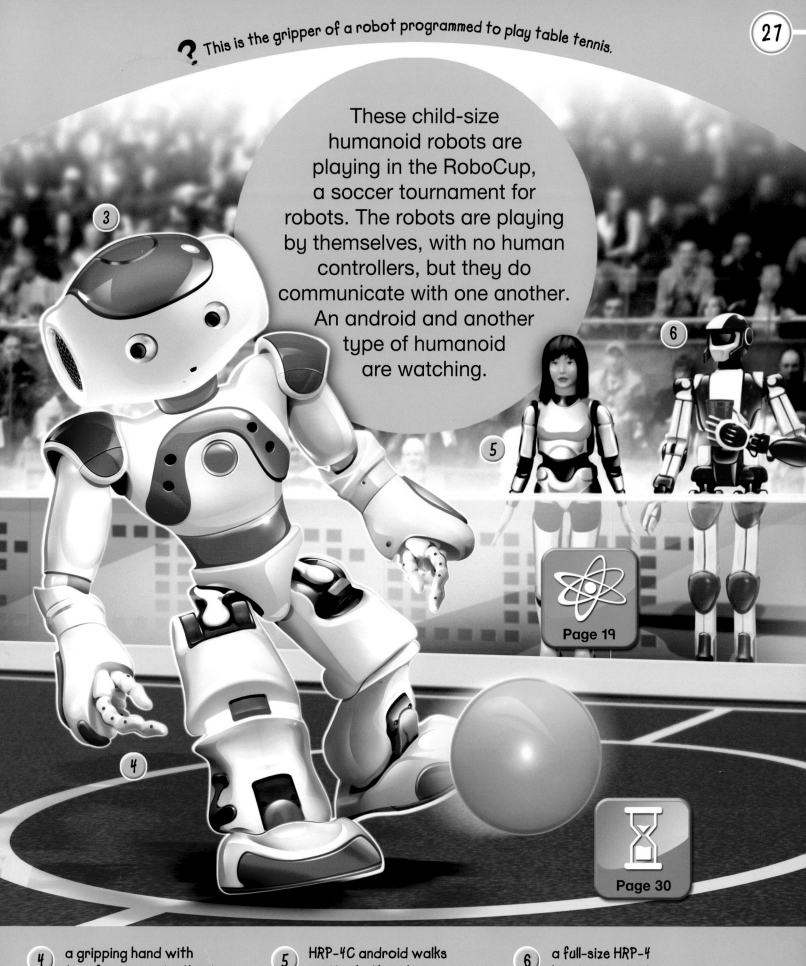

? This is the gripper of a robot programmed to play table tennis.

These child-size humanoid robots are playing in the RoboCup, a soccer tournament for robots. The robots are playing by themselves, with no human controllers, but they do communicate with one another. An android and another type of humanoid are watching.

3

4

5

6

Page 19

Page 30

4 a gripping hand with two fingers and a thumb

5 HRP-4C android walks and looks like a human.

6 a full-size HRP-4 humanoid robot

Page 19
Page 30

Robot or human?

Engineers are creating robots that look, move, sound, and behave like humans. The latest androids have facial expressions. From a distance, you might think they are real people!

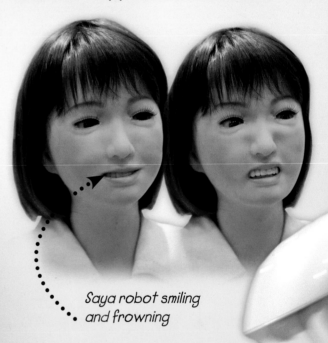

the mechanisms inside the head of a Saya robot

One of the most lifelike robots so far is Geminoid-F (below, on the right). It has silicone skin that is realistic to look at and touch, and it makes superrealistic facial expressions.

To communicate feelings, androids have mechanisms in their heads. These change the shape of their faces so they can create expressions such as happiness or sadness.

Saya robot smiling and frowning

Musical-instrument-playing robots have been built. The skills scientists learn by building these complex machines help make advances in the science of robotics.

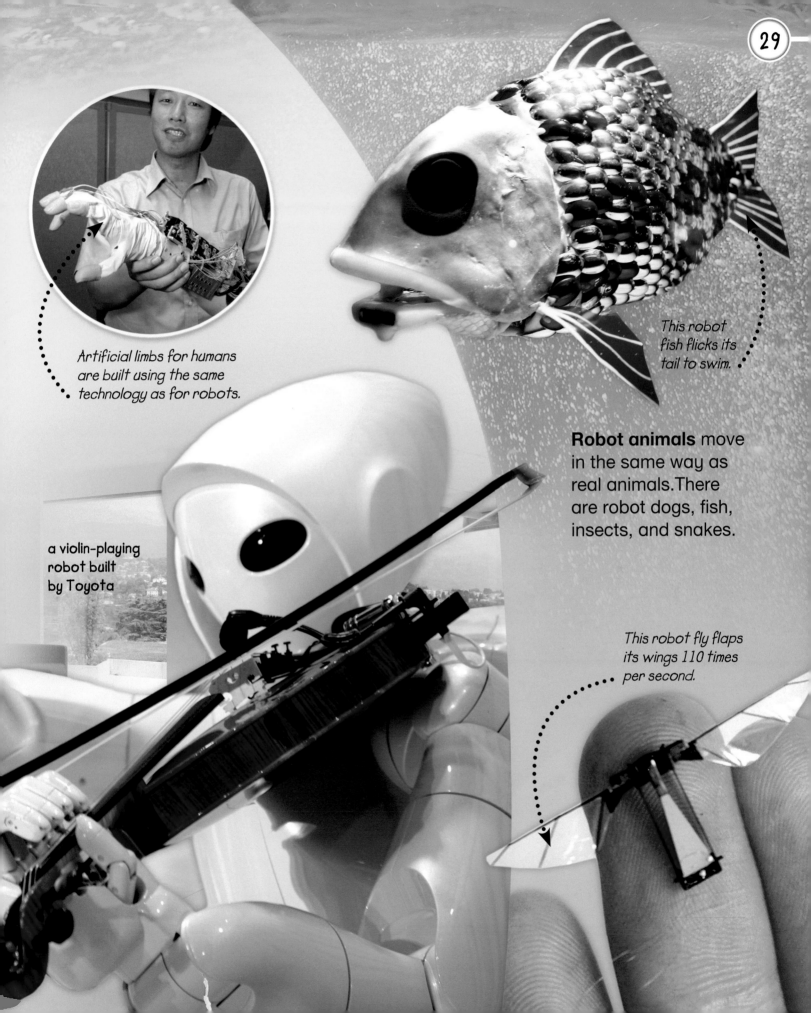

Artificial limbs for humans are built using the same technology as for robots.

This robot fish flicks its tail to swim.

Robot animals move in the same way as real animals. There are robot dogs, fish, insects, and snakes.

a violin-playing robot built by Toyota

This robot fly flaps its wings 110 times per second.

Argo

History

In 1985, **Argo**, a remotely operated vehicle, discovered the wreck of the *Titanic* at more than 12,800 ft. (3,900m) below the surface of the Atlantic Ocean. The 16-ft. (5-m) craft was designed by explorer Robert Ballard.

Lunokhod 1 was the first successful mobile space probe. It landed on the Moon in 1970 and drove across the Moon's surface taking photos and analyzing the soil.

SUGV robot

Science

Submersible robots, such as the **ABYSS** AUV (autonomous underwater vehicle), are used to explore the ocean floor. In 2011, ABYSS found the wreckage of an airplane.
ABYSS

Tracks on a robot provide more friction than wheels—this helps the robot grip rough ground.

Technology

Mobile robots go further because of improvements in **battery technology**. An alternative to batteries are fuel cells. They create electricity from a chemical reaction.

fuel cells

The Curiosity rover has this **nuclear power source** onboard. It is expected to create enough electricity to run the probe's systems during its mission on Mars.

FRIDA

Future

Luna

This may be the look of helper robots to come. Meet **Luna**, a human-size robot with a touchscreen, sensors, and WiFi, that can be controlled using smartphone-style apps.

Future industrial robots, such as the **FRIDA** experimental robot, will have two arms to hold and work on objects.

More to explore

The first industrial robot was **Unimate**. It began work at the General Motors factory in 1961, moving and welding parts.

As early as the 1600s, Japanese inventors built robotlike mechanical dolls called **Karakuri**. They were designed to entertain guests by writing on paper or serving tea.

Experimental android robots such as **HRP-4C** help scientists understand how people interact with machines that look and act like humans.

The **Curiosity rover's** mission involves analyzing samples of Martian soil to determine whether there was once life on Mars.

Curiosity

Robotic machine tools are linked to **computer-aided design** and **manufacturing** systems. The tools cut and shape metal parts. Here a robot arm is loading unfinished pipe joints into a machine tool.

Images taken underwater by remotely operated vehicles (ROVs) are sent along **fiberoptic cables** to a control room on a ship.

ExoMars rover

It will be decades before human astronauts visit Mars. Until then, rovers such as **Curiosity** and the upcoming **ExoMars** are the future of space exploration.

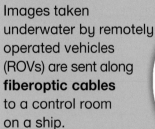

computer model of Cheetah

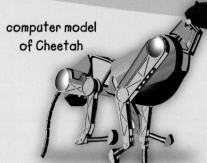

The fastest robot is the **Cheetah**. Engineers hope to build a version in the future that can run as fast as a real cheetah—about 70 mph (110km/h).

Index